DOWN TO EARTH!

What's Up with the Weather?
A Look at Climate

TRACI STECKEL PEDERSEN

PERFECTION LEARNING®

Editorial Director:	Susan C. Thies
Editor:	Mary L. Bush
Design Director:	Randy Messer
Book Design:	Michelle Glass, Lori Gould
Cover Design:	Michael A. Aspengren

A special thanks to the following for his scientific review of the book:
Jason Parkin, Meteorologist, KCCI Weather, Des Moines, IA

Image credits:
Corbis (Rights-Managed): p. 21 (bottom)

Corbis (Royalty-Free): p. 12 (top); MapArt: pp. 6, 7, 8, 10, 11; Photos.com: cover, all chapter numbers, all background images, pp. 1, 4, 5, 9, 12 (bottom), 13, 14, 15, 16, 18, 20, 21 (top), 23, 24

For information, contact
Perfection Learning® Corporation
1000 North Second Avenue, P.O. Box 500
Logan, Iowa 51546-0500.
Phone: 1-800-831-4190
Fax: 1-800-543-2745
perfectionlearning.com

1 2 3 4 5 6 PP 10 09 08 07 06 05

Paperback ISBN 0-7891-6610-0
Reinforced Library Binding ISBN 0-7569-4634-4

Table of Contents

chapter 1
Weather That Lasts

Imagine you're going on a vacation to Hawaii. You pack your suitcase full of shorts, T-shirts, and swimming suits. Now imagine your surprise if the weather forecaster suddenly announced that it's snowing in Hawaii.

Or what if you're going on a trip to Alaska? Your suitcase is stuffed with jeans, sweatshirts, and jackets. Then suddenly you hear that temperatures in Alaska just reached 100°F.

Why are these situations just imaginary? Because over time, we've come to expect certain places in the world to have

Hawaii

Alaska

Arizona

certain kinds of weather. We expect the tropical islands of Hawaii to be hot all year long. We also know that Alaska will have a long, cold winter and a cool summer. Why is this? Because every place in the world has a specific **climate**. A climate is the normal, or usual, weather in an area. It's weather that has lasted for hundreds or thousands of years.

The climate in an area includes its sunlight, **humidity**, temperatures, **precipitation**, and winds. Different types of climates are found all over the world. Some are hot and rainy. Others are cold and dry. And there are many other combinations in between. These climates create different types of **habitats** such as hot rain forests, dry deserts, and frozen **tundra**.

So the next time you and your family plan a vacation, think about the climate where you're going—and be sure to pack the right stuff!

chapter 2

A Recipe for the Weather

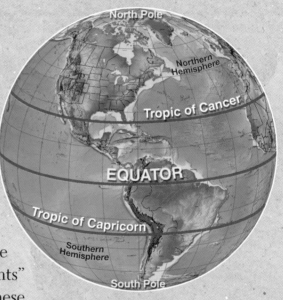

Have you ever followed a recipe to cook or bake something? If so, then you know that you need the right ingredients for the recipe to turn out the way you expect. The same is true of climates. Each climate is produced when the right mixture of "ingredients" comes together in an area. These climate ingredients are sunlight, wind, ocean **currents**, and the water and land features in an area.

Where in the World Is the Sunlight?

If you look on a globe, you'll notice lines running around it.

What are these lines? They are lines of **latitude**. Certain lines of latitude have special names. The line in the middle of the globe is called the **equator**. The Tropic of Cancer is a line of latitude north of the equator. The Tropic of Capricorn is a line of latitude south of the equator.

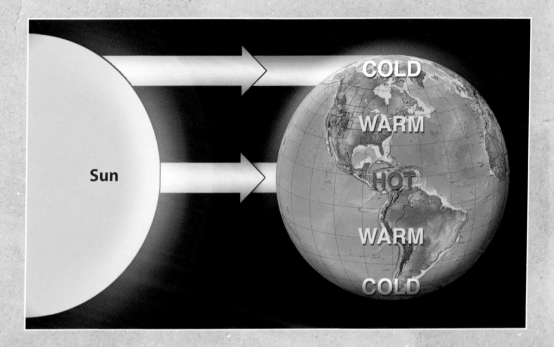

An area's latitude has a big effect on its climate because it determines how much direct sunlight the area receives. The land at the equator (between the Tropic of Cancer and the Tropic of Capricorn) receives the most direct sunlight. This means that places located close to the equator have hot climates year-round. This area is known as the **tropics**.

The farther you move north or south of the tropics, the less direct sunlight the Earth receives. This means that the climate is cooler. The areas in the middle of each **hemisphere** have warm climates. They usually have seasons. The summers are warm, and the winters are cool.

The poles never receive direct sunlight. This is why the North and South Poles have very cold climates all year long.

Blowing in the Wind

Local **winds** are part of your everyday weather. Some days you feel almost no wind. Other days the wind is gusting around you.

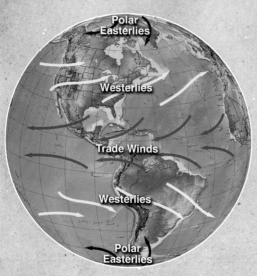

Global winds

Global winds help determine climates. Global winds are steady patterns of air movement that occur across the world. They carry warm air away from the equator. They push cold air away from the **poles**. When warm or cold winds pass over an area, they affect the air temperature. When warm winds meet cold winds, storms often form.

Water Weather

Ocean currents are the flow of water in a certain direction. They are steered by winds and the spinning of the Earth. Like winds, ocean currents help carry warm water away from the tropics and cold water away from the poles. Land near warm currents is usually warmer and rainier. Land bordered by cold currents usually has drier, cooler weather.

The Gulf Stream is an important warm ocean current. It carries tropical warmth from the Caribbean Sea to western Europe.

The Humboldt Current is a cold-water current. This current carries icy water from Antarctica along the southern and western coasts of South America. Because of this chilly current, seals and penguins are able to live in the tropics of South America.

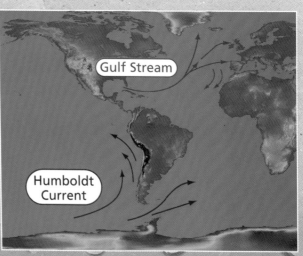

From the Oceans to the Mountains

Almost three-fourths of the Earth is covered by oceans. Water cools down and heats up more slowly than land. So climates near oceans have smaller differences between their winter and summer temperatures.

The altitude, or height above sea level, of an area affects its climate. Higher altitudes have cooler temperatures. So two cities in the same latitude may have very different temperatures if one city is higher than the other. For example, Denver, Colorado, and Philadelphia, Pennsylvania, are at about the same latitude. But Denver is more than 5000 feet higher in altitude. So Denver has cooler average temperatures than Philadelphia.

This change in temperature with altitude also influences climate on mountains. The climate on a tall mountaintop might be cold and snowy, while the bottom of the mountain is a tropical rain forest.

The climate on one side of a mountain may be very different from the climate on the other side. As warm air rises to cross over a mountain, it cools and releases any water it carries. So the land on this side of the mountain may get lots of rain. By the time the air has reached the other side of the mountain, all of the precipitation has fallen. So this side of the mountain may be a dry desert.

Chapter 3
Turning Up the Heat

If you like hot weather, then about half of the world's climates are for you. Of course, some of these climates are hotter than others. And some are hot and wet, while others are hot and dry. Each warm climate has its own characteristics.

Ice cap	Polar	Subarctic	Dry (Semiarid)
Highland	Continental moist	Oceanic moist	Desert
Subtropical dry summer	Subtropical moist	Tropical wet and dry	Tropical wet

Tropical Wet

The tropical wet climate is hot and humid year-round. You definitely don't need a jacket since the average temperature is about 80°F. A raincoat would be useful, though, because more than 70 inches of rain falls each year.

This type of climate is found in tropical rain forests near the equator. The warm, wet weather is great for leafy green trees and plants.

Tropical rain forest

Tropical Wet and Dry

The tropical wet and dry climate has hot temperatures year-round too. However, this climate has two seasons—one wet and one dry. Some places in this climate experience **monsoons** in the summer. These strong winds bring heavy rains that can cause terrible flooding.

In October, the winds turn and blow in the other direction. This is the beginning of the dry winter season.

In areas that don't receive as much rain during the summer, savannas form. Savannas are open grasslands with bushes and a few trees.

Subtropical Moist

The subtropics are the areas right outside the Tropic of Cancer and the Tropic of Capricorn. These areas have warm tropical weather during the summer but cooler weather during the winter.

Key West, Florida, has a subtropical moist climate.

The subtropical moist climate is found on the eastern side of continents, next to the oceans. The warm, wet air from over the oceans provides steady rainfall and humidity throughout the year.

The Meaning of *Moist*

Several climates have the word *moist* in them. What does this word mean? *Moist* means slightly damp or wet. Moist climates get a steady amount of precipitation throughout the year.

Subtropical Dry Summer

The subtropical dry summer climate has warm, dry summers followed by mild, wet winters. You can find this climate in southern California, southwestern Australia, and countries around the Mediterranean Sea.

Italy lies along the Mediterranean Sea.

Utah desert

Dry (Semiarid)

The dry, or semiarid, climate has warm to hot summers and very cold winters. Only 4–20 inches of precipitation falls each year. The land in dry climates is often covered by **steppes**. These grasslands are often found next to deserts.

Desert

With less than 10 inches of precipitation each year, deserts are the driest climates. These climates can fall both in and out of the tropics. The temperatures in deserts can vary. Some deserts have hot days and nights. Others have hot days and cold nights. A few have hot and cold seasons. It is not the temperature, but the extreme dryness, that makes a climate a desert.

chapter 4
You're Getting Colder

If you'd rather live with penguins and polar bears, then you'd prefer the cooler climates of the world. These climates vary from cool and rainy to freezing and icy.

Oceanic Moist

Coastal lands far from the equator have an oceanic moist climate. Areas with this climate are in the path of winds that blow cool, moist ocean air across the land. Rainy, foggy, and cloudy days are very common. Being near the ocean also helps keep the temperatures less extreme. This makes summers comfortably warm and winters cool but not frigid.

San Francisco, California

Jordon Pond, Maine

Continental Moist

As you move away from the ocean coast, the climate changes to continental (land) moist. Without a nearby ocean, there are bigger differences between summer and winter temperatures. The seasons are very noticeable. **Deciduous** trees thrive in the summer and then lose their leaves in the fall. Snow is very common in the winter. The northeastern United States has a continental moist climate.

Highland

The highland climate is found in high mountains and **plateaus**. The precipitation and seasons on a mountain are the same at the top and bottom of the mountain. The higher you climb, however, the colder the temperature is. So although it's summer or winter on the entire mountain, it's a much cooler summer or winter at the top.

A mountain slope might actually have several different climates on it. For example, a mountain in a tropical wet climate may have rain forests at the bottom and cooler grasslands and forests higher up.

The highland climate is found on mountain ranges such as the Rockies in North America, the Andes in South America, and the Himalayas in Asia.

Andes Mountains

Alberta, Canada

Subarctic

As you move farther north into Canada and the northern parts of Europe and Asia, cold temperatures become a way of life. Summers are short and cool. Winters are long and very cold. Snow begins in the fall and lasts through early summer. Rain falls during the brief summer. Forests of conifer trees stand tall in this chilly climate.

Polar

Brrr! It gets even colder above the subarctic. The polar climate, or tundra, is a dry, cold climate found on the lands bordering the Arctic Ocean. There won't be any pool parties here because even summer temperatures stay below 50°F. The cold temperatures keep water from **evaporating** and forming clouds, so rain and snow are very light.

A lot of the ground here is frozen most of the time. During the short summer, the top layer of soil may thaw out so grasses can grow. No trees can survive in the harsh land.

Newfoundland tundra

Ice Cap

The ice cap climate is just like its name. It's a cap of ice and snow on the top and bottom of the Earth. Temperatures in this climate are always below freezing. The lowest temperature ever recorded on Earth was in Antarctica—a frosty -128.6°F.

You might think that such a cold place would have a lot of snow, but it's actually so cold that it hardly snows at all. In fact, scientists call these areas "polar deserts" because they receive as little precipitation as other deserts. So why is there so much ice then? Because when it does snow, the snow never melts.

The ice cap climate receives very little sunlight. For six months out of the year, the Sun doesn't even appear in the sky. The Sun is very low the other six months. Even during the "warmer" months, the sunlight is reflected off the icy white surface. That's why it never gets any warmer and the ice never melts.

Inquire and Investigate: Reflecting Heat

Question: Do light or dark surfaces reflect more heat?

Answer the question: I think that _____ surfaces reflect more heat.

Form a hypothesis: (Light/Dark) surfaces reflect more heat.

Test the hypothesis:

Materials
- white T-shirt
- black T-shirt

Procedure
- Lay both T-shirts on the ground outside on a warm day. Make sure they are sitting in a spot that gets full sunlight. Wait a few minutes. Feel the shirts. Which one feels cooler?

Observations: The white T-shirt feels cooler.

Conclusions: Light surfaces reflect more heat. This is why the icy poles stay cold and frozen. Much of the heat from the Sun is reflected back into space.

chapter 5 Changes in Climate

Lucky for you and your vacation plans, climates don't normally change quickly. You can pretty much count on wearing shorts in Hawaii and pants in Alaska. However, throughout history, the Earth has experienced some unusual weather. And slow changes in climate have taken place over time.

The Little Ice Age

From the 1350s to the 1850s, many parts of the world went through a long "cold spell." This was known as the Little Ice Age. The ice age was especially hard on people living in Europe and North America. Winters were terribly cold. Rivers froze. Glaciers grew larger and covered farms and villages. Many people died from lack of food.

Scientists are still trying to figure out what caused the Little Ice Age. Two possibilities are a decrease in the Sun's activity and an increase in volcanic activity. If the amount or strength of the

sunlight reaching the Earth changed, it could have affected the temperatures on the planet. The ash thrown into the air from strong volcanic eruptions could have blocked out the Sun and covered the ground. This would have made it colder and prevented crops from growing.

El Niño

Hundreds of years ago, fishermen from Peru noticed that every few years, warm water from the equator would flow into their cold fishing waters. The men called this event El Niño.

During El Niño, the warmer water temperature adds heat and moisture to the air. All of these changes bring weather that differs from normal. Usually, the weather is hotter and wetter. But sometimes, El Niño brings **drought**. Scientists are still not sure what causes El Niño, but they continue to learn more about it and its effects on climate.

Scientist of Significance

In the early 1900s, many scientists were trying to understand El Niño. Sir Gilbert Walker, however, was studying monsoons in India. He was trying to figure out how to predict when monsoons would occur. His research led him to believe that the monsoon winds were connected to droughts in some parts of the world and warmer winters in other parts.

Walker was the first person to suggest that weather was a global occurrence. At the time, most scientists believed that the weather in one place in the world had nothing to do with the weather on another part of the planet.

Walker's discoveries were ignored for 50 years. Then, in the 1960s, other scientists began to realize the connection between El Niño and world weather patterns. Finally, Walker's important theories gained the attention they deserved.

The Greenhouse Effect and Global Warming

Have you ever been inside a greenhouse? If you have, then you know that it's a hot spot. The glass windows allow light to enter but keep most of the heat from escaping. This is similar to what happens on Earth. Certain gases in the atmosphere work like those glass panels. They allow light to pass through and trap enough heat to keep us warm.

But over the past 100 years, the atmosphere seems to be trapping more heat than usual. The Earth has heated up about 1°F. Some scientists believe that this is because people are releasing more heat-trapping gases, such as carbon dioxide, into the atmosphere. This warming of the atmosphere is called the *greenhouse effect*.

Scientists don't know for sure what will happen if the Earth continues to heat up. But they have made predictions. Higher temperatures could melt glaciers. Hotter temperatures also make water expand, or take up more space. These two events could cause oceans to overflow and flood surrounding land. Warmer temperatures could also threaten animals such as polar bears and

greenhouse gases in the air could help. Recycling puts less garbage in landfills. Planting trees reduces the amount of carbon dioxide in the air since trees use this gas to make food.

✿✿✿✿✿✿✿✿✿✿✿✿✿✿✿✿✿

You may like it hot and humid or cold and snowy. Where you live and where you vacation are often determined by the climate. Changes in this climate could bring big changes to your life. Now that you know "what's up with the weather," you can make better choices about how you affect the climate and how climate may affect your future.

penguins that depend on cold environments.

What can be done to stop **global warming**? Factories, cars, landfills, and power plants all release greenhouse gases into the air. Reducing the amount of

Technology Link

What kind of car might help prevent global warming? A hybrid car! Hybrid cars use two or more types of power. Many use a combination of gas, batteries, and electricity. These cars have smaller engines that are less wasteful than the bigger engines in regular cars. They are more energy efficient and release fewer greenhouse gases into the atmosphere.

Internet Connections and Related Reading for Climate

http://www.epa.gov/globalwarming/kids/index.html
What's the difference between weather and climate? And what does it have to do with the greenhouse effect and global warming? Find out at this Environmental Protection Agency site for kids.

http://www.coolkidsforacoolclimate.com/
Become a cool kid who works for a cool climate. Learn more about the changes in the world's climate and what actions can be taken to help.

http://uk.oneworld.net/penguin/global_warming/climate_home.html
Tiki the Penguin introduces you to climates, the greenhouse effect, and global warming. He also suggests ways you can help stop harmful climate changes.

http://www.blueplanetbiomes.org/climate.htm
Get the facts on climate. Then use the map and the brief descriptions of each type of climate to explore climates around the world.

❖❖❖❖❖❖❖❖❖❖❖❖❖❖❖

Experiments with Weather by Salvatore Tocci. A collection of experiments on weather. Crabtree Publishing, 2003. ISBN 0-5162-7809-6 (PB) 0-5162-2790-4 (CC). [RL 4.6 IL 3–5] (6870801 PB 6870806 HB)

Meteorology: Predicting the Weather by Susan and Steven Wills. Meet seven scientists who measured the weather, observed its patterns, and developed ways to predict it. Oliver Press, 2003. ISBN 1-8815-0861-7. [RL 5 IL 4–8] (3544806 HB)

Weather and Climate by Alvin and Virginia Silverstein and Laura Silverstein Nunn. Explains the fundamental concepts of weather and climate, gives some background, and discusses current developments. Millbrook Press, 1998. ISBN 0-7613-3223-5. [RL 5 IL 5–8] (3112506 HB)

What Will the Weather Be? by Lynda DeWitt. Explains the basic characteristics of weather and how meteorologists gather data for their forecasts. HarperCollins, 1993. ISBN 0-0644-5113-5 (PB) 0-0602-1596-8 (CC). [RL 3 IL K–4] (4426301 PB 4426302 CC)

- RL = Reading Level
- IL = Interest Level

Perfection Learning's catalog numbers are included for your ordering convenience. PB indicates paperback. CC indicates Cover Craft. HB indicates hardback.

Glossary

climate (KLEYE mit) usual weather in an area over a period of time

current (KER ent) flow of air moving in a certain direction

deciduous (dee SIDJ you uhs) type of tree that sheds its leaves in the fall

drought (drowt) long period of extremely dry weather

equator (ee KWAY ter) imaginary line running around the middle of the Earth

evaporating (ee VAP or ay ting) changing from a liquid to a gas

global warming (GLOH buhl WAR ming) increase in the world's temperatures

habitat (HAB i tat) place where a plant or animal lives

hemisphere (HEM uhs sfear) half of the Earth

humidity (hyou MID uh tee) amount of moisture in the air

latitude (LAT uh tood) imaginary lines that circle the globe horizontally

monsoon (mahn SOON) strong wind that changes directions seasonally and produces heavy rainfall

plateau (plat OH) hill or mountain with a flat top

pole (pohl) top or bottom of the Earth

precipitation (pree sip uh TAY shuhn) moisture that falls to the ground as rain, snow, hail, etc.

steppe (step) dry, treeless grassland

tropics (TRAH piks) area between or near the Tropics of Cancer and Capricorn where the weather is warm year-round

tundra (TUHN druh) area of permanently frozen topsoil where no trees grow

wind (wind) moving air

Index